D1493713

stopping the
pain

---

a workbook for teens
who **cut & self-injure**

LAWRENCE E. SHAPIRO, PH.D

Instant Help Books
A Division of New Harbinger Publications, Inc.

Publisher's Note

This publication is designed to provide accurate and authoritative information in regard to the subject matter covered. It is sold with the understanding that the publisher is not engaged in rendering psychological, financial, legal, or other professional services. If expert assistance or counseling is needed, the services of a competent professional should be sought.

Distributed in Canada by Raincoast Books

Copyright © 2008 by Lawerence E. Shapiro
Instant Help Books
A Division of New Harbinger Publications, Inc.
5674 Shattuck Avenue
Oakland, CA 94609
www.newharbinger.com

Cover and text design by Amy Shoup

Printed in the United States of America

ISBN-13: 978-1-57224-660-7

The Library of Congress has cataloged the trade edition as:

Shapiro, Lawrence E.
  Stopping the pain : a workbook for teens who self-injure / by Lawrence E. Shapiro.
    p. cm.
  ISBN-13: 978-1-57224-602-7 (pbk. : alk. paper)
  ISBN-10: 1-57224-602-2 (pbk. : alk. paper)
  1. Self-mutilation in adolescence--Juvenile literature. I. Title.
RJ506.S44S53 2008
616.85'8200835--dc22

                                    2007051985

14   13   12

10   9   8   7   6   5   4   3

contents

to the professionals reading this book

I have designed this workbook as a practical tool to facilitate therapy by a trained counselor and not as a substitute for counseling. The activities can be done with teens as part of counseling sessions, or they can be sent home as psychological homework. Many of the activities ask teens to think about difficult problems and feelings, and teens will likely need extra emotional support when doing those activities.

The activities primarily deal with the symptom of self-injurious behavior, but they also touch on possible underlying causes, such as early trauma, and comorbid disorders, such as depression and eating disorders. A thorough assessment is always necessary to determine the appropriate range of services for each teen.

Counselors should be aware that there are a variety of service settings for teens who self-injure and also several distinct treatment models. The most common treatment approaches include cognitive behavioral therapy, dialectical behavior therapy, group therapy, and medication for depression and/or anxiety. Even though most teens who self-injure say that they are not making suicide attempts with their self-injury, when depressive symptoms are present, the possibility of suicide is always an issue. In addition, there may be significant health risks associated with the methods teens are using to self-injure, and these must be addressed as part of treatment.

- Treating teens who self-injure requires that therapists consider the following:

- Their ability to make a long-term commitment to the patient

- The availability of ongoing support and supervision

- Their personal availability to teens who are in crisis

- Their commitment to maintaining a nonjudgmental attitude toward the client, no matter how disturbing the behavior

Self-injury is now recognized as a widespread problem of teens as well as adults, affecting an estimated 1 percent of the population. With the increasing attention to this problem, more resources are becoming available every year. Recommended books include:

Treating Self-Injury: A Practical Guide, by Barent W. Walsh, Guilford Publications, 2005

The Scarred Soul: Understanding & Ending Self-Inflicted Violence, by Tracy Alderman, New Harbinger Publications, 1997

Bodily Harm: The Breakthrough Healing Program for Self-Injurers, by Karen Conterio and Wendy Lader with Jennifer Kingson Bloom, Hyperion Books, 1998

Cognitive-Behavioral Treatment of Borderline Personality Disorder, by Marsha M. Linehan, Guilford Publications, 1993

There are many reasons why teens self-injure, but the behavior itself is always disturbing. Fortunately, with our increasing knowledge of this problem, dedicated professionals can make a significant difference.

to the teens reading this book

If you are reading this book, it is likely someone thinks that you have a problem with self-injury and that this workbook can help.

While there are many reasons why you self-injure, I'm sure you know that hurting yourself is not a good way to deal with your problems. My purpose in writing this workbook is to give you a better way to cope with your troubling thoughts and feelings. But for this workbook to be of any benefit, you must be ready to try to stop hurting yourself.

If you want to stop hurting yourself, this workbook can help you:

- Understand why you hurt yourself

- Find better ways to handle difficult feelings

- Control your desire to hurt yourself

- Make a commitment to stop hurting yourself and get the right kind of support you need from the people who care about you

This book will not take the place of counseling. People who hurt themselves on an ongoing basis need the support of an experienced counselor, and you should make every effort to stay connected to someone you trust to help you. This workbook will not only help you better understand yourself, but it can also help your counselor understand you, which should result in many benefits.

You may find that some of the activities can trigger troubling thoughts and memories. You should talk to your counselor about the things that upset you, whatever they may be.

It is an unfortunate truth that life is often full of pain, both physical and mental. We all experience pain throughout our lives, but you don't have to make things worse for yourself. I hope this workbook will help you find healthier ways to cope with the things that bother you. It will take a lot of effort, but I know that it will be worth it.

Sincerely,

Lawrence E. Shapiro, Ph.D.

section 1

getting ready to help yourself

Making the decision to get help for yourself is not an easy thing to do. If you are like most teens who self-injure, this habit has become a way for you to cope with difficult feelings, and it might be hard to imagine getting through a week without relying on it.

While this workbook is designed to help you "stop the pain" of self-injury (SI), it is also designed to help you better cope with your emotional pain, including the pain of being alone with your problem.

Learning to stop your self-injury is a lot like learning to stop other addictive behaviors. It takes a strong desire to stop and a commitment of your time and energy, and it also takes a lot of support from other people.

In this first section, we will lay the groundwork for finding better ways to cope with your problems and to lead a happier and healthier life. You will take the first steps in learning to trust others with your secret of SI, and you will also examine the role SI plays in your life.

what you say is private

you need to know

What you write in this workbook or what you tell a counselor is private. No one will know about your thoughts and your feelings unless you want them to. The only exception is if your life is in danger, because saving your life is more important than protecting your privacy.

Sometimes counselors will want to talk to your parents or even your teachers about your problems. If they want to do this, they should ask your permission first. If they talk without your knowing, it may be hard for you to trust them.

If you like, you can ask your counselor, or other people you confide in, to sign the confidentiality statement on the next page. It will help people understand that your privacy is important.

Counselor's Confidentiality Form

I agree to keep what I am being told confidential and private. Even if I don't like what I'm hearing, I will not repeat it unless I have your permission.

However, if I think you are doing something that will put you or someone else in real and immediate danger, I will do whatever I can to stop something bad from happening.

I also want you to know: _____

_____

_____

_____

_____

_____   _____
(Therapist 's Name)   (Date)

you need to know

Very few adults are comfortable talking about self-injury, and many teens keep their self-injury secret. They think that it will "freak out" their parents, and they are afraid that their parents or other adults will act in ways that make things worse. Many teens are ashamed or guilty about their SI and feel that there is something wrong with them. Naturally, they don't want other people to think they are crazy.

Most teens keep their SI secret from their parents, and when parents find out about it, they typically keep it secret from other people in the family.

But keeping your SI secret doesn't help you and probably makes your situation worse. Keeping SI, or any other problem, secret makes you feel alone, and when you feel alone, you are more likely to feel depressed and helpless. For teens who self-injure, these feelings can lead to even more self-injury.

Of course, telling a secret to people who don't want to hear it is a real problem. Many teens say:

"If I tell my parents, they won't be able to handle it."

"If I tell my therapist, she'll probably put me in a hospital."

"If I tell my friends about my SI, they will just tell an adult about it."

These things may all be true, but if you are ready to get help with your SI, then telling people your secret should be part of your asking for help. Everyone reacts differently when someone asks for help.

On the next page fill in the blanks and cross out sentences that you don't agree with or that don't apply to your situation.

Then use the statements you like as the basis for writing a letter to your parents about your SI. You don't have to give your parents this letter; that is up to you. You can give it to someone else or you can tear it up as soon as you write it. But even if you tear it up, you should think about what you have written and how you might want to share it with people you care about and people who care about you.

Dear _____

I don't want you to freak about what I'm going to tell you, but I need your help. If you freak out, you won't be able to give me the help I need. I want to tell you a secret that I've had for _____.
Sometimes when I feel _____. I hurt myself. I hurt myself by _____.

I know that it is hard to understand, but when I do this I feel _____

_____.

There is nothing that you have to do right now. I just want to talk to you, and I want you to know that I need your help. The best thing you can do to help me right now is to _____.

I also want you to understand that self-injury is a problem that will need your understanding and patience.

Thanks for helping me.

Signed,

_____

Use the space on the next page to write a letter to your parents or to another adult who can help you with your SI. You can use sentences from the first part of this activity or you can create your own.

3   what do you know about si?

you need to know

People have many myths and misconceptions about those who self-injure. The more you know about self-injury, the quicker you will find a way to help yourself.

Most people who self-injure keep their behavior secret. They might feel that they are the only ones in the world who act this way. Even people who are seeing counselors may be ashamed to admit that they hurt themselves.

In the last few years, more people have talking about self-injury, and it has become less secret. Many books have been written about self-injury. There are also many websites and blogs, although it is important for you to be aware that not everything you read on the Internet is in your best interest.

The more people talk about self-injury, the more we can understand how to help people with this problem. Separating myths from facts is always a step in the right direction. You may want to take the "quiz" on the next page yourself or give it to someone else.

what do you know about people who self-injure?

Put a check next to the statements that are true and an X next to the ones that are false. The answers are on the next page.

1. Only a few very sick people self-injure.

2. Teens who hurt themselves are trying to commit suicide, but they don't have the nerve.

3. There are many ways that people self-injure.

4. People who self-injure are crazy and should be put in hospitals.

5. Teens who self-injure are just trying to get attention from their parents.

6. Self-inflicted wounds are a way of being accepted at school.

7. Only teens who have other serious psychological problems will harm themselves.

8. If your wounds are superficial, your self-injury may be just a phase.

9. Girls and boys typically self-injure in different ways.

answers

1. *Only a few very sick people self-injure.* **FALSE**
   Approximately 1 percent of the population has, at one time or another, used self-inflicted physical injury as a means of coping with an overwhelming situation or feeling.

2. *Teens who hurt themselves are trying to commit suicide, but they don't have the nerve.* **FALSE**
   While some teens who self-injure are also suicidal and think often about death, most teens say that when they self-injure they are not trying to die. Most say that their self-injury is a way of coping with the pain in their lives, and some say that it has become just a habit.

3. *There are many ways that people self-injure.* **TRUE**
   Self-injury is defined as intentionally hurting yourself. People find many ways to do this, but most commonly they cut or burn their skin.

4. *People who self-injure are crazy and should be put in hospitals.* **FALSE**
   According to Tracy Alderman, author of The Scarred Soul, most self-inflicted wounds are not life threatening and may not even require medical attention. Some teens are put in a hospital for a short period because the adults in their lives are afraid and don't know what else to do. Experts in this field have suggested that hospitalization can actually make matters worse. Most teens who hurt themselves are trying to find control in their lives, and involuntary hospitalization makes them feel worse, potentially leading to even more self-injury.

5. *Teens who self-injure are just trying to get attention from their parents.* **FALSE**
   Some teens say that they began to self-injure when they were trying to get attention for their emotional troubles, but when they thought about it, they realized that their behavior was really a silent cry for help and not designed to attract attention. In fact, the majority of teens who hurt themselves go to great

lengths to hide their scars and their behaviors from adults, particularly their parents. Many professionals believe that all psychological symptoms are ways of trying to get help, but the symptoms are often so disguised that people don't recognize them for what they are. That is, of course, a big part of the problem.

6. *Self-inflicted wounds are a way of being accepted at school.* **FALSE**
While some teens will form a clique with other teens who self-injure, very few teens say that they harm themselves just to be a part of a group. There is an expression that "misery loves company," and it is more likely that teens who are unhappy find comfort in being around other teens with similar feelings.

7. *Only teens who have other serious psychological problems will harm themselves.* **FALSE**
While it is true that some teens who self-injure do have other very serious problems, which they may have had for many years, this is certainly not the case with everyone. You can find more about the reasons that you self-injure in Activity 4.

8. *If your wounds are superficial, your self-injury may be just a phase.* **FALSE**
The severity of self-injury has very little to do with the feelings you might have. People have different tolerances to pain and they have different ways to hurt themselves. When teens hurt themselves, it should be taken seriously.

9. *Girls and boys typically self-injure in different ways.* **TRUE**
While it is true that girls more commonly fall into a pattern of self-injury, there are many boys who do this too. Some people think that girls who self-injure are just found out more often than boys. Others think that boys are more indirect in seeking self-injury and are more likely to hurt themselves through high-risk behaviors, such as extreme sports.

thinking about yourself

Was there any information in the answers that surprised you? If so, tell what it was.

_____

_____

_____

What are some other false beliefs that people have about self-injury?

_____

_____

_____

What are some false beliefs that people have about you?

_____

_____

_____

_____

Who is the person that knows you the best? Do you think that person knows about your self-injury?

_____

_____

_____

_____

4   why do people hurt themselves?

you need to know

Many people have a hard time understanding or even talking about self-injury because it seems so unnatural to them. Understanding why pain can feel good can help people understand why you self-injure.

While most people think of pain as a bad thing and something to avoid, everyone has had some experience with pain feeling good. Here are some examples of pain that can feel good:

- Firmly massaging an aching muscle

- Scratching an itch

- Diving into a cold lake or pool on a 95-degree day

- Taking a whirlpool bath in hot water

- Vomiting when you are nauseated

- Popping a pimple

- Exercising even though your muscles burn

Some scientists believe that a sudden pain, as opposed to a prolonged ache, releases endorphins, a biochemical that produces a kind of high in the brain. This is one explanation of why self-injury may be addictive for some people.

There are also psychological reasons why pain might feel good. On the next page, you will find some reasons that teens give for self-injury. Circle the one or two that best describe the reasons why you self-injure.

why do you self-injure?

I hurt myself, because it is the one thing in my life I can control.

I hurt myself because it keeps me from feeling numb and dead inside.

I hurt myself because it is better than thinking about all the bad memories I have.

I hurt myself because I deserve to be punished.

I hurt myself because it's exactly the kind of thing that would upset my parents the most.

I hurt myself because it makes me feel things that I can't put into words.

thinking about yourself

What would your life be like if you didn't self-injure?

_____

_____

_____

_____

Who is the one person you think can most understand what you are feeling?

_____

What are some of the feelings that you have just before you self-injure?

_____

_____

_____

What things do you do immediately after you self-injure?

_____

_____

_____

_____

are you ready to stop hurting yourself? 5

People don't stop bad habits just because others don't like what they do. There are many reasons why you hurt yourself. You are the only one who can understand those reasons, and you will only stop your SI when you are ready. But how will you know when you are ready?

This workbook includes many ideas that can help you stop your self-injury and deal with some of the problems in your life that make you want to hurt yourself, but none of this advice will do any good until you decide that you are ready to stop hurting yourself. It is not easy for any of us to change our behavior or our feelings, but making a commitment to change is the first step.

rating your readiness to change

Rate each statement below from 1 to 10, with 1 = "I don't agree" and 10 = "I strongly agree." Most people who are ready to stop their self-injury, or break any habit, are ambivalent about change, so don't expect to get a score of 100.

Hopefully, as you learn ways to conquer your SI, your motivation to change will increase, so you may want to rate your readiness every week or two to see if your score changes.

_____ I want to completely stop hurting myself.

_____ I want to make new friends.

_____ I want to treat my body better.

_____ I want to have a better relationship with my parents.

_____ I want to be open and honest when I need help.

_____ I want to develop a healthy lifestyle.

_____ I want to find positive things in my life that make me happy.

_____ I want to wake up each day glad to be alive.

_____ I want to have a positive plan for the future.

_____ I want to have a lot of people in my life whom I can care about and who care for me.

Total Score _____

thinking about yourself

Have you ever accomplished something you thought you couldn't? What happened?

_____

_____

_____

_____

Do you know someone who you consider highly motivated? How does that person stay motivated?

_____

_____

_____

Have you ever broken a difficult habit? How were you able to do it?

_____

_____

_____

Many people are motivated by reward, something that they will get when they achieve a goal, but even more people are motivated by approval from others. Who in your life will give you the most positive feedback and approval when you stop hurting yourself?

_____

section 2

thinking about yourself and your si

For most people, self-injury and other addictive behaviors are ways to avoid thinking about problems. As you learn more about yourself and the way you handle your problems, it should be easier to stop your self-injury.

Learning about yourself is a lifelong process. Your friends, your family, and where and how you live will constantly change as you grow older. You will change, too. Every day, you have the opportunity to make choices that can make your life happier and more fulfilling. As you develop insight about yourself, you will find it easier to make better choices and to deal with stresses and problems.

what is your self-image? 6

you need to know

There are many aspects to your self-image. People are very complex, with virtues and faults. A large part of your self-image comes from how much attention you pay to your positive versus your negative qualities. People with good self-images pay more attention to their positive qualities and believe that they have control over their problems.

Most people who self-injure have a poor self-image. Many teens say that they hurt themselves because they think they deserve to be punished. Some teens hurt themselves because they were emotionally or physically hurt when they were younger. Although it doesn't seem rational, some people say they feel better when they are repeating the hurt they experienced when they were younger.

If you have a poor self-image, you can improve it. The more you learn to find things that you like about yourself, the less you will want to hurt yourself.

activity 6 ✳ what is your self-image?

your ten best qualities

What are your positive qualities? List your ten best qualities here:

1. _____

2. _____

3. _____

4. _____

5. _____

6. _____

7. _____

8. _____

9. _____

10. _____

Now complete the second part of this activity to find out what others see as your best qualities.

asking others about your best qualities

Ask three people you like and respect to each tell you what they think are your three best qualities. Whether or not you agree, write those qualities here:

Feedback from Person 1:

_____

_____

_____

Feedback from Person 2:

_____

_____

_____

Feedback from Person 3:

_____

_____

_____

Now rate each person's feedback from 1 to 7, depending on how much you agree with it. Put a 1 if you think that you don't have this quality at all and put a 7 if you strongly agree that you possess this positive quality.

thinking about yourself

Was it hard for you to think about your positive qualities? If it was, tell why.

_____

_____

Was it hard for you to hear others talk about your positive qualities? _____

Was there one person who seemed to know you best? _____

_____

Some people find it hard to accept praise and positive feedback. Think about whether you discredited what you heard or were able to accept that people saw positive things about you that you may not have seen.

Write one positive thing you heard that you know is true.

_____

_____

Write one positive thing you heard that you think is true but that you aren't really sure about.

_____

_____

Write one positive thing you heard that you would like to be true even though you don't believe it really is.

_____

_____

you can change yourself if you want to

you need to know

An important part of having a positive self-image is believing that you can change the things about yourself that you consider to be problems. Hurting yourself is certainly one of these things, but there might be others as well.

Everyone has things that they want to change about themselves. Of course, there are some things that we can't change about ourselves, like our height or our body type, but there are many more things that we can change.

what do you want to change about yourself?

Write five things that you want to change about yourself.

1. _____

2. _____

3. _____

4. _____

5. _____

Now rate whether you think you can change this problem. Next to each, put a number from 1 to 7, with 1 = "I can't change this problem" and 7 = "I'm confident that I can change this problem."

If you didn't give yourself high ratings in this exercise, don't be discouraged. If you have a poor self-image, you may have unrealistic expectations of yourself or you may lack the self-confidence to think that you can change.

In Activity 26: *Setting Goals for Yourself Will Help You Stop SI*, you will learn how to set goals for yourself, which will help you change your life if you really want to.

thinking about yourself

What is one thing about yourself that you do not want to change?

_____

_____

If you know someone who has recently made a positive change in his or her life, tell what that person changed. How did the change happen?

_____

_____

_____

_____

Think of something that you would like to change in your life and then think of someone who can help you make that change. What would be the most helpful thing that person could do for you?

_____

_____

_____

_____

8 what is your body image?

you need to know

Most teens who self-injure have poor body images. Some teens say that they scar and hurt themselves because they don't like their bodies, but, of course, harming themselves just makes them feel worse. When you learn to treat your body better, you will be taking an important step in recovering from your SI.

Some teens say that intentional scarring is no different from tattooing or piercing their bodies, but this argument is not logical. The reasons people self-injure are different from the reasons they get tattoos. People who get tattoos are proud of them and like to call attention to them, but people who self-injure are ashamed of what they have done and keep their scars hidden. By definition, self-injury involves harming yourself; it does not involve other people, like tattoing or piercing do.

It is important to understand that whenever the skin is broken, there are real health risks, particularly from blood-borne diseases including hepatitis B and C, tetanus, and HIV-AIDS. The greatest risks occur when people break the skin using objects that are not properly sterilized.

Like people who have eating disorders (see Activity 33: *Facing Your Problems Around Food*), many people who self-injure have distorted views of their bodies. They may think that parts of their bodies are really ugly when they are not, and they almost always have a hard time accepting their bodies as they are.

This activity includes four exercises to help you think about your body image and how it relates to your SI.

which parts of your body do you like and which parts don't you like?

On the picture below, use a blue crayon or marker to show the areas of your body that you like. Use a red crayon or marker to show the areas you don't like.

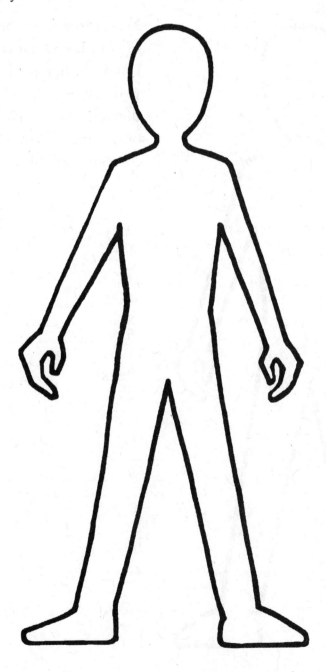

which parts of your body do you self-injure?

On the picture below, use a pencil to draw scars you have inflicted on yourself or to show places you have harmed yourself in other ways.

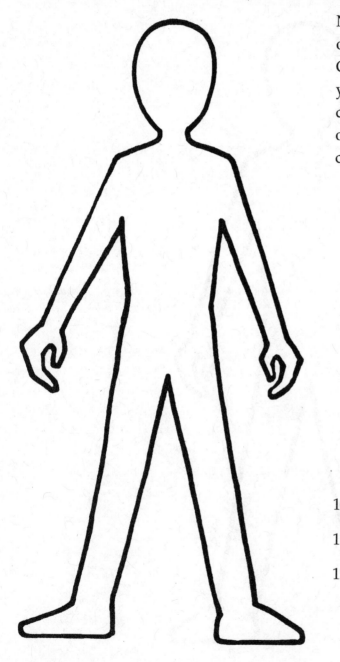

Now, place a number next to each part of your body that you want to change. Can you change them without hurting yourself, perhaps through exercise or diet, or by a change in fashion, hairstyle, or make-up? Write "yes" or "no" on the corresponding lines below.

1. _____

2. _____

3. _____

4. _____

5. _____

6. _____

7. _____

8. _____

9. _____

10. _____

11. _____

12. _____

In the column on the left, list the names of the body parts you think you can change without hurting yourself. In the column on the right, rate how motivated you are to change that body part, with 1 = "not really motivated" and 10 = "extremely motivated."

Body Part	How Much I Want to Change

Finally, make a plan to change the body parts that you just rated 6 or higher. Think of a person who can help you with this plan and of how you can carry it out. Remember that a healthy diet and regular exercise are hard habits to maintain. You may need a lot of support in changing eating and exercise patterns, and you will need to develop good coping skills to deal with setbacks. (See Activity 28: *Coping with Stress.*)

_____

_____

_____

_____

_____

_____

_____

_____

_____

_____

_____

_____

can you treat your body better? 9

you need to know

Learning to treat your body better is an important step on your road to recovery from self-injury. Spending just a few minutes each day making your body feel good will improve your mood and lead to healthier ways of coping with stress.

Self-injury has become a habit for you, and habits are hard to break. But you can also develop the habit of being good to your body. It may seem strange, but you can have two opposing habits at the same time. You can develop the habit of doing things that enhance the beauty and pleasure of your body even while you might feel like doing things that make your body unattractive or cause pain.

Hopefully you will soon find that being good to your body feels more natural than hurting it.

treating your body better

Put a circle around ways that you think you can be good to your body. Circle only the things you would actually do.

Self-massage

Take a bubble bath

Exercise

Moisturize your skin

Meditate

Get your nails done

Take a walk along a beach or another restful place

Add other ideas here:

_____

_____

_____

In the chart on the next page, write the things you circled. Since it takes about a month to form a new habit, make at least four copies of your chart. Try to do at least two of these things every day, checking them off after you do them. The more you get into the habit of making your body feel better, the closer you will be to overcoming your SI.

good-habit chart

Things That Make My Body Feel Good	M	Tu	W	Th	F	Sa	Su

10 understanding why you self-injure

Here is the story of one girl who self-injures. Read it and then think about your personal history.

When I was about twelve, I accidentally cut myself with some scissors. I was using the scissors to open an envelope, and they slipped and made a long gash up my arm. The pain was horrible. A few months later I was at a party, and a girl who I thought was my best friend wouldn't even say hello. Then I saw two other girls who also ignored me. I stood there trying to talk to them, and it was like I was a ghost or something.

The next day, I asked another girl why everyone was ignoring me. She said it was because I looked like a freak and I had freaky-looking hair, and those other girls were into the preppy thing.

I wasn't trying to be a freak or anything, but I couldn't afford the preppy clothes that my friends—make that former friends—were wearing. I kept thinking about those girls and the party and how I felt like an invisible ghost and stuff, and then I saw the scissors on the table and remembered when I had cut myself.

I thought, well if I look like a freak, I might as well be a freak, so I picked up the scissors and cut my arm. Although all the stinging hurt, I just had this thing where I liked the pain and I liked to watch myself bleed.

I tried to stop because I knew it was wrong, and I eventually got better. But in the 7th or 8th grade, it started up again. Sometimes when I wanted to punish myself, I'd put a little bit of salt in my cut, or put milk, orange juice, salt, and vinegar in a cup, put a cap on the cup, shake it up, and then I'd drink it. And then of course, I'd throw up. Which is another thing I like.

I've also put a toothbrush in the back of my throat until I threw up. I've lighted candles as an attempt to calm myself, but I couldn't help but leave my finger in the flame until I got a blister or something. It's gotten worse to the point where I shut everyone out and I am stuck in my own little world. I've gotten so desperate that now if I want to cut at school, I can use a piece of wire from a spiral notebook and scratch. Sometimes I put peroxide on my cuts and watch it foam. I bite my tongue or the inside of my mouth too, until I bleed. The doctor has been trying to get me to stop for a while, and I haven't hurt myself for one month.

a self-injury questionnaire

What do you have in common with the teen who wrote this story?

_____

_____

_____

_____

_____

_____

What are some differences between you and the teen who wrote this story?

_____

_____

_____

_____

What are some thoughts you have about this story?

_____

_____

_____

_____

Is there a lesson behind this story?

_____

_____

_____

If the girl who wrote this story were in your school, would she be someone you'd be friends with? Why or why not?

_____

_____

_____

_____

are you like other people who self-injure? 11

you need to know
Teens who self-injure may have different reasons for doing it, but they often share a similar way of looking at themselves and their world.

Self-injury is a behavior that is hard for many to understand, but people who self-injure often have similar thoughts and feelings, and even similar backgrounds.

How much are you like other teens who self-injure? On the next page you will find a questionnaire that asks you to compare yourself to other teens who self-injure. The higher the score, the more you are like other teens who have this problem.

self-injury questionnaire

The statements below are commonly made by people who self-injure. Rate each statement from 1 to 5, with 5 = "strongly agree" and 1 = "strongly disagree."

_____ I am very critical of myself.

_____ I am very sensitive to rejection.

_____ I am angry almost all the time but I usually hide my anger.

_____ When I want to do something that I know I shouldn't, I have a hard time controlling myself.

_____ I like the way my blood looks.

_____ I rarely think about the future.

_____ I am depressed almost every day.

_____ When I hurt myself, I feel like I am watching myself in a movie. It just doesn't seem quite real.

_____ I had a terrible childhood.

_____ A lot of things make me worried and anxious.

_____ People always bother me.

_____ When I get even a little stressed, I start to fall apart.

_____ I try to avoid people and situations that upset me.

_____ I don't think anyone really understands me.

_____ I hurt myself because it makes me feel in control.

thinking about yourself

Do you think you are similar to other teens who self-injure? If so, how?

_____

_____

What are some of the important ways that you think you are different from other teens who self-injure?

_____

_____

_____

What are some ways you are different from teens who don't self-injure?

_____

_____

_____

Who do you know that is most like you? Explain your answer.

_____

_____

_____

12 describing your si

> # you need to know
>
> Thinking about how your self-injury started may help understand how it became a habit in your life. It might also help your counselor understand you better.

Now it is time to describe your self-injury. Some teens find that it is easy to talk about their SI, and others find it very difficult. Even if you find it easy to talk about your SI, you may learn something from this exercise.

You may or may not find this exercise helpful, but it will definitely help your counselor in understanding your SI.

the facts about your self-injury

1. What age were you when you began to self-injure? _____

_____

2. Describe the first time you remember hurting yourself on purpose. _____

_____

3. How often do you self-injure? _____

_____

4. What do you use to hurt yourself? _____

_____

5. What parts of the body do you injure? _____

_____

6. How do you feel before, during, and after you self-injure? _____

_____

_____

7. Have you ever tried to stop your SI? What happened? _____

_____

_____

8. Who knows about your SI? _____

_____

9. What kinds of situations make you want to self-injure? _____

_____

10. What kinds of things do you do to stop your SI? _____

_____

_____

11. When do you think you will be able to completely stop your SI? _____

_____

_____

thinking about yourself

Which of the questions in this activity were difficult for you to answer? _____

_____

_____

_____

What feelings did these questions bring up? _____

_____

_____

_____

In the space below, write something about your SI that wasn't asked in this activity.

_____

_____

_____

_____

_____

_____

_____

you are much more than a 13
person who self-injures

> ## you need to know
>
> When people have problems, those problems sometimes become the most important thing to them as well as to others. But people are complex, and there are many aspects of you that are more important than the fact that you self-injure. When you start paying attention to other aspects of yourself and your life, you may find it easier to stop hurting yourself.

We tend to think about people in simple terms, categorizing them by their most obvious traits. Maybe you know someone who is deaf or extremely tall or short or who has a stutter. If you know a person with an obvious physical difference well, you know that the difference is only a small part of who that person is.

So just who are you? Let's forget for a moment that you self-injure. Fill in the questionnaire on the next page to reveal some other aspects of yourself. You will clearly see that this questionnaire focuses on the positive aspects of yourself and your feelings. This may seem strange, but research tells us that thinking in more positive terms and being more optimistic is an important part of your recovery.

about me

My height is _____.

My weight is _____.

My favorite subject in school is _____.

My favorite teacher is _____.

My favorite TV show is _____.

My all-time favorite movie is _____.

My all-time favorite book is _____.

One place I'd like to go is _____.

One thing I really like about my family is _____.

One thing I like about my best friend is _____.

My favorite sport is _____.

One hobby that I like is _____.

My best quality is _____.

thinking about yourself

In the space below, write five positive things about yourself or your life.

1. _____

_____

_____

2. _____

_____

_____

3. _____

_____

_____

_____

4. _____

_____

_____

5. _____

_____

_____

14 understanding your feelings

you need to know

The more you understand about the feelings that make you want to hurt yourself, the closer you will be to finding better ways to solve your problems.

Sometimes it is easy to understand why you feel a certain way. If someone gives you a compliment, you will probably feel happy. If someone says or does something rude to you, you will probably be angry. If someone you care about has a problem, you will probably be worried or upset.

At other times, feelings come for no apparent reason. On a beautiful, bright spring day, you might feel depressed even though nothing is really wrong. You might wake up feeling angry and irritable and yet not have any real reason for feeling this way. Sometimes our emotions seem to have lives of their own. Yet if you stop to think about your feelings, you will often find a pattern.

Most teens say that they hurt themselves as a way to control their upsetting feelings. An important part of recovering from SI is learning to understand all your feelings and finding better ways to cope with the ones that upset you.

In this activity, you will get a chance to think about all the feelings you are capable of having and which ones you most commonly have.

what are your primary feelings?

As you can see by the list below, humans are capable of hundreds of shades of feelings. However, most of us have ten or twelve feelings that we commonly experience throughout a day. Circle the feelings below that you commonly have. Circle as many feelings as you like.

abandoned, abused, accepted, accused, admired, adventurous, affectionate, affirmed, afraid, aggravated, aggressive, agitated, alarmed, alienated, alive, alone, ambivalent, angry, annoyed, antagonistic, anxious, apathetic, appreciated, apprehensive, arrogant, ashamed, assertive, attacked, attractive, awed, awkward

balanced, beaten-up, belligerent, betrayed, bewildered, bitter, blamed, bored, bothered, bugged, burned up

capable, cared for, caustic, chagrined, challenged, cheated, closed-up, comfortable, comforted, compassionate, competent, complacent, compromised, concerned, confident, confused, controlled, out of control, creative, cruel, crushed, curious, cut off

deceived, defeated, defensive, defiant, degraded, dejected, delighted, deserving, desired, desperate, devastated, dirty, disappointed, discontented, disgusted, disillusioned, dismayed, distant, distorted, distracted, distressed, disturbed, dominated, domineering, drained, dreadful, drugged, dumb

eager, edgy, elated, embarrassed, empty, endangered, enraged, enthused, envious, exasperated, exhausted, exhilarated, exploited, explosive, exposed

like a failure, fat, fatigued, fearful, fighting mad, floundering, fooled, forgiven, forgotten, foul, free, friendly, frightened, frustrated, furious

galled, generous, genuine, gifted, gracious, grateful, gratified, greedy, grumpy, guilty

happy, hated, healed, heavy, helpless, hopeful, hopeless, hostile, hurt, hyperactive, hypocritical

ignored, immobilized, impatient, impotent, inadequate, incompetent, in control, indecisive, independent, indifferent, indignant, inferior, infuriated, inhibited, injured, insecure, irked, irritated, isolated, integrated, intense, intimate, intimidated, irrational, irritated

51

jealous, joyful, judged, judgmental

liberated, light, limited, lonely, like a loser, lost, lovable, loved, loyal

mad, manipulated, melancholic, miffed, misinformed, misunderstood

naked, needy, neglected, noxious

obligated, offended, optimistic, outraged, overlooked, oversized, overwhelmed

pained, panicked, paranoid, passionate, peaceful, persecuted, perturbed, pessimistic, phony, pissed off, playful, pleased, possessed, possessive, powerful, powerless, precious, preoccupied, pressured, private, protective, proud, provoked, punished, purposeful, put down, put out, puzzled

ragefilled, rambunctious, reassured, rejected, resentful, responsible, responsive, restrained, reverent, rewarded, rigid

sad, sadistic, scapegoated, scared, secretive, secure, seething, selfish, sensual, shaky, shamed, shocked, shy, sick, sincere, sinful, smothered, soiled, sorrowful, spontaneous, spiteful, stressed, strong, stubborn, stupid, subservient, superior, supported, suspicious, sympathetic

tender, terrified, threatened, ticked off, tired, tolerant, tolerated, traumatized, tranquil, triumphant, trusted, trusting, turned off

ugly, unable, unappreciated, unbalanced, uncertain, understood, unfulfilled, unhappy, unique, unlikable, unloved, unprepared, upset, unresponsive, uptight, used, useful, useless

valuable, vengeful, vicious, vindicated, vindictive, violent, vulnerable

warm, weak, weary, whole, withdrawn, wonderful, worn out, worthless, worthy

yearning

zany, zealous

Write other feelings here: _____

_____

thinking about yourself

Were you surprised by any of the feelings you circled? _____

Read the list again and put a line under feelings you used to have but rarely have now. Why do you think your feelings have changed?

_____

_____

_____

What are the three feelings that you have most often? _____

_____

Describe a time in your life when you had more of the positive feelings you circled.

_____

_____

_____

_____

_____

15 what causes your feelings?

you need to know

There are usually patterns to your feelings and your behaviors. Understanding when you have upsetting feelings and how you cope with them will help you better understand your SI. Understanding what triggers your positive feelings may help you learn what you can do that will keep you in a better mood.

Your upsetting feelings, as well as your positive ones, occur for predictable reasons. They may be triggered by outside events, such as when someone you know is mad at you, or by internal thoughts or memories. Feelings are also influenced by things we take for granted, like the weather, the season, the time of day, the food you eat, how much sleep and exercise you get, and so on.

Although you can never have complete control of your feelings, you can learn to manage them better, coping with distressing feelings more effectively and increasing your positive feelings.

This activity will help you identify the feelings you commonly have and then keep track of them throughout the day.

your feelings throughout the day

On the chart on the next page, write how you feel during each hour you are awake. The chart covers twenty-four hours, because some people get up early and some stay up late. You can put a line through the hours when you are sleeping.

Refer to the feelings you circled in Activity 14: *Understanding Your Feelings*, and try to be as specific as possible in identifying your feelings. Rate how strong each feeling was, with 1 = "not a very strong feeling" and 10 = "a very powerful feeling." Then write what you were doing when you had the feeling.

activity 15 * what causes your feelings?

Time	Feeling	Strength	What Were You Doing
6 a.m.			
7 a.m.			
8 a.m.			
9 a.m.			
10 a.m.			
11 a.m.			
noon			
1 p.m.			
2 p.m.			
3 p.m.			
4 p.m.			
5 p.m.			
6 p.m.			
7 p.m.			
8 p.m.			
9 p.m.			
10 p.m.			
11 p.m.			
midnight			
1 a.m.			
2 a.m.			
3 a.m.			
4 a.m.			
5 a.m.			

After you have completed this chart for a day, answer the questions on the next page.

what did you learn about your feelings?

Which feelings did you have most often?

_____

_____

_____

Which feelings were the strongest?

_____

_____

_____

Did any particular event usually trigger your positive feelings?

_____

_____

_____

Did any particular event usually trigger your unpleasant feelings?

_____

_____

_____

Think about whether this was a typical day. If it wasn't, you may want to complete the chart again.

16 faulty thinking can contribute to feelings of helplessness and despair

you need to know

Your thoughts have a lot to do with the way you feel. If you have a negative, pessimistic outlook, you will tend to see the things that support this point of view, and not see things that might make you feel more positive. But if you change the way you think, then you can see your life in more positive terms, which can help you feel better.

Therapists know that most emotional problems are caused in part by faulty "automatic" thoughts. These automatic thoughts are considered to be faulty because they are not based in fact, but rather on misconceptions and distortions of the importance of things in your world.

There are ten kinds of distorted automatic thoughts that therapists believe are responsible for emotional disorders. They are the following:

1. **All-or-Nothing Thinking:** You see things in black-and-white categories. If your performance falls short of perfect, you see yourself as a total failure.

2. **Overgeneralization:** You see a single negative event as a never-ending pattern of defeat.

3. **Mental Filter:** You pick out a single negative detail and dwell on it exclusively. Like a drop of ink that discolors an entire beaker of water, this type of thinking darkens your vision of all reality.

4. **Disqualifying the Positive:** You reject positive experiences by insisting that they don't count for one reason or another. In this way, you can maintain a negative belief that is contradicted by your everyday experiences.

5. **Jumping to Conclusions:** You make a negative interpretation even though there are no definite facts that convincingly support your conclusion, by one of the following:

A. **Mind Reading:** You arbitrarily conclude that someone is reacting negatively to you, and you don't bother to check out your conclusion.

B. **The Fortune-teller Error:** You anticipate that things will turn out badly and you feel convinced that your prediction is an already established fact.

6. **Magnification or Minimization:** You exaggerate the importance of things, such as your mistake or someone else's achievement, or you inappropriately shrink things until they appear tiny, for example, your own desirable qualities or other people's imperfections. This is also called the "binocular trick."

7. **Emotional Reasoning:** You assume that your negative emotions necessarily reflect the way things really are: "I feel it, therefore it must be true."

8. **"Should" Statements:** You try to motivate yourself with "should" and "shouldn't," as if you had to be punished before you could be expected to do anything. "Musts" and "oughts" are also offenders, and the emotional consequence is guilt.

9. **Labeling and Mislabeling:** This is an extreme form of overgeneralization. Instead of describing your error, you attach a negative label to yourself, such as "I'm a loser." When someone else's behavior rubs you the wrong way, you attach a negative label to that person: "He's an idiot." Mislabeling involves describing an event with language that is highly emotionally loaded.

10. **Personalization:** You see yourself as the cause of some negative external event, which in fact you were not primarily responsible for.

On the next page, you will find an exercise that may help you identify the types of faulty automatic thoughts that are common to people who self-injure.

learning to identify the faulty thinking of si

These are common automatic thoughts that many self-injurers have. In the column on the right, write the type of faulty thinking that underlies each statement, using the list from pages 60 and 61. Some statements may represent more than one type of distorted thinking.

Automatic Thought	Type of Thought Distortion
No one understands how I feel.	All-or-nothing thinking
Hurting myself is the only way I can control my feelings.	
I deserve to be hurt.	
I'm a freak, so I might as well look like one.	
When I hurt myself, I feel alive.	
If I hurt myself, it really doesn't hurt anyone else.	
I am fat and/or ugly, and this is how I show I hate my body.	
Pain feels good.	
I like the way blood on my body looks and feels.	
Hurting myself is the best way to get back at my parents.	
When I scar myself, I can see the terrible history of my life.	
Cutting myself is just like getting a piercing or a tattoo.	
People from many cultures see body marking as a source of pride. It's no big deal.	
Hurting myself is preferable to throwing up and to other things I have done.	
Hurting myself is just a bad habit, like smoking, and I can stop if I want to.	
I know lots of people who hurt themselves, and they are perfectly normal kids who do well in school.	
I've read about a lot of famous people who hurt themselves and still became rich and successful.	
I hurt myself because I was hurt when I was little, and it is just what I am used to.	

you can correct your 17
automatic thoughts

you need to know

Counselors and therapists believe that most emotional problems are fed by irrational thoughts and faulty thinking. Irrational thoughts are ways that we think that are not based on facts, but rather on misconceptions and misperceptions. The problem is that these irrational thoughts often become automatic over time.

Irrational thoughts are also called "automatic thoughts" because they come to us in a split second, triggered by a situation, a person, or even a memory. Therapists believe that if you can change your automatic thoughts, you can change your feelings and even your behavior.

It takes a lot of practice to be able to "catch" your automatic thoughts and change them into realistic thoughts, but if you learn to do this, it will be an important step on your road to recovery and you will be able to apply this skill to many areas of your life.

In this activity, you will learn to think about your automatic thoughts: how they come to you and how you can replace them with more realistic, fact-based thinking. Use these instructions to fill in the columns on the next page:

- Write down the situation that triggered the negative thoughts.

- Identify the moods that you felt in the situation.

- Write down the automatic thoughts you experienced when you felt the mood.

- Identify the evidence that supports these automatic thoughts.

- Identify the evidence that contradicts the automatic thoughts.

- Observe your mood now and think about what you are going to do.

Situation (Trigger)	Your Feelings	Automatic Thoughts	Evidence That Supports These Thoughts	Evidence That Contradicts These Thoughts	Mood Now

thinking about yourself

What is the one type of automatic thinking that you most often have? _____

_____

_____

_____

What is the one thought you have that is most illogical and untrue? _____

_____

_____

_____

Which automatic thoughts happen just before you hurt yourself? _____

_____

_____

_____

Which automatic thoughts do you think you can most easily change?_____

_____

_____

_____

18 doing things that will make you happy

"Anhedonia" is the word for not being able to find pleasure in things that would normally make you happy. It is from the Greek *hedon*, and it is the opposite of hedonism, a philosophy that sees pleasure as the primary purpose of life.

Finding pleasure in everyday things is an important step on your road to recovery. Although this may seem obvious, and even simplistic, it may not be as easy to do as you think.

On the next page, you will find a list of activities that most teens find pleasurable. As you read the list, consider whether your thoughts and feelings about these activities have changed over the years. The chart on page 65 can help you keep track of how many pleasurable activities you do in a week.

pleasurable activities checklist

Check off the things below that you enjoy or used to enjoy. Add as many other pleasurable activities as you can think of:

_____ Movies

_____ Parties

_____ Sports

_____ Surfing on the Internet

_____ Going to a bookstore

_____ Shopping

_____ Reading

_____ Listening to music

_____ Playing music

_____ Hiking

_____ Biking

_____

_____

_____

_____

_____

_____

increasing your pleasurable activities

In the chart below, write in at least five activities that you used to enjoy. Make copies of this chart to use for four weeks. Now see how many pleasurable activities you can do in a week. Put a check mark each time you do one. Put a number by each check mark to indicate how much you enjoyed the activity, with 1 = "not at all" and 10 = "very enjoyable." Then total your score for each day and at the end of the week.

Activity	M	Tu	W	Th	F	Sa	Su
Total							

Weekly Total _____

See if you can increase the number of pleasurable things that you do, as well as your enjoyment of each activity, each week.

thinking about yourself

Is there one person you know with whom you enjoy doing pleasurable activities? Can you spend more time with that person?

_____

What is one pleasurable activity that you can do every day?

_____

Is there a pleasurable activity that has an almost instant effect on your mood?

_____

What keeps you from doing pleasurable activities more often?

_____

_____

19 avoiding things you can use to hurt yourself

you need to know

When you are ready to stop your SI, you need to start avoiding the things that you use to hurt yourself.

If you are a cigarette smoker who wants to quit, you will certainly not want to have cigarettes anywhere near you. If you are trying to build healthy eating habits, you don't want to have a kitchen full of ice cream, cookies, and snacks high in calories. Similarly, if you are in the habit of cutting, burning, or hurting yourself in other ways, then you don't want to be around the things you commonly use to hurt yourself.

It is impossible to avoid everything you might use to hurt yourself. But most teens who self-injure use the same things each time, and you can certainly make an effort to stay away from objects such as scissors, matches, or razor blades.

Making the effort to avoid the things that you use to hurt yourself is an important step on your road to recovery.

Make a list of the things you use to self-injure, noting where each one is now and where you can put it so that it will not be around when feel like hurting yourself. Certain objects that you might use will be hard to avoid, but you can still keep from having them close at hand.

Objects You Use to Hurt Yourself	Where They Are Now	Where You Can Put Them To Make Them Harder To Use on an Impulse

thinking about yourself

What might prevent you from making the commitment to keep away from things you use to hurt yourself?

_____

_____

_____

Who can help you stay away from those things? Think of as many people as you can.

_____

_____

_____

What thoughts go through your mind when you feel like hurting yourself? List them below.

_____

_____

_____

When you have the urge to hurt yourself, try to control it for as long as you can, and notice how long it takes to go away. In the space below, rate how strong your urge is for each five-minute period, with 5 = "I can barely control my urge to hurt myself" and 1 = "It is not a big deal."

Minutes	Rate Your Urge
5	
10	
15	
20	
25	
30	
35	
40	
45	

20 what you can do instead of hurting yourself

you need to know

Many teenagers find that they can resist the impulse to hurt themselves if they do some other activity. Psychologists call these "replacement activities." You can find a replacement activity that makes you think less about hurting yourself and do that activity until your impulse to self-injure goes away.

The best way to reduce your SI is to plan on doing another activity at the time and place that you prefer to hurt yourself. You should try to do these replacement activities several times a week, even when you don't have the urge to self-injure. Then, when you get the impulse to self-injure, immediately start on a replacement activity.

These are some of the activities that teens say can help keep them from hurting themselves:

- **Journal Writing:** Writing about your feelings will also help by allowing you to see your problems more clearly.

- **Relaxation Techniques:** There are many ways to relax, such as yoga or listening to quiet music. Try going for a walk around your neighborhood or meditating. Focus on your breathing and think of calming, pleasant things.

- **Music and Dance:** Listening to your favorite music, singing, or dancing can be relaxing as well as giving you an outlet for pent-up emotion.

- **Art:** Painting, drawing, or working with clay can be very therapeutic.

- **Reading:** Reading a good book can be a great way to distract yourself from self-injury.

- **Exercise:** Exercise of any sort can help distract you from self-injury, and it is healthy in its own right. Exercise can be as simple as taking a walk.

- **Gardening:** Gardening can be very relaxing for some people. Even in the winter, you can cultivate an indoor garden.

- **Aromatherapy:** Many people find aromatherapy an effective technique to ease stress and reduce anxiety. There are kits available that let you design your own aromatic candles and perfumes.

- **Cleaning your closet or organizing your desk.**

- **E-mail and Instant Messaging:** Many teens love to communicate with other teens they know, and even those they don't know, through e-mail, instant messaging, and blogs. For this activity to serve as a replacement, you should avoid conversations about your SI or sites about SI. Always be aware that there are people using the Internet who wish to harm teens; you should never give our your name, phone, address, or any personal information to a stranger.

how successful is your replacement activity?

In the chart below, keep track of your mood as you do a replacement activity. Rate each activity on a scale of 1 to 5, with 1 = "not successful" and 5 = "very successful."

Replacement Activity	Success Rating

thinking about yourself

Are there any activities that you used to enjoy but have stopped doing? Can you take these up again?

_____

_____

Most activities are more enjoyable when they are shared. List three people you might ask to do different replacement activities with you.

_____

_____

_____

What replacement activity are you most likely to use? What could prevent you from using this activity to avoid hurting yourself?

_____

_____

Some teens use replacement activities that mimic their SI habits. For example, they might draw on their bodies with red markers instead of cutting themselves. Other teens say that these kinds of activities just make them think about their SI and don't really help. What do you think?

_____

_____

_____

section 3

✳

connecting with others

Many teens turn to self-injury because they feel alone, misunderstood, and powerless to make themselves feel better. Creating a personal connection with other teens or adults will be an important part of your recovery.

In this section, you will learn ways to connect with others by communicating your feelings, your problems, and your needs. Connecting with others is something you need to think about every day.

Of course, talking about SI is a lot different from talking about other aspects of your life. As you know, some people will find it hard to hear about your SI, and they may react in ways that you find upsetting. Hopefully, the activities in this section will make it easier for you to talk to people about your SI and get the kind of support you need.

talking with people about who you really are 21

you need to know

Once you have started to talk about your SI, you will probably find that you have a lot to say. But it is important to keep in mind that SI is a behavior, something you do. Your SI is not who you are. Who you are—your personality—is made up of your feelings, your interests, your likes and dislikes, your fears, your hopes and dreams, and your experiences.

Some teens say that they self-injure because they don't like who they are. They may be unhappy and lonely. They may not like the way they look. They may have had something bad happen in their families or with their friends that they can't forget.

Most of the time, you will feel better if you talk about who you are with someone who cares about you. Hopefully, you are seeing a counselor or a therapist you trust. Counselors are trained to help you talk about your feelings and to sort them out, but there are probably other people that you know who can do this, too.

Before you can open up about your feelings, you have to trust the person you are talking with. You might want to review Activity 1: *What You Say Is Private* and Activity 2: *SI Does Not Have to Be a Secret* before you begin this activity.

Talking about their innermost thoughts and feelings is a difficult thing for most people, not just for people who self-injure. But once you start talking about your feelings, it is very likely that you will feel better.

In this activity, you will begin by listing people, other than your therapist, with whom you think you can talk about your thoughts and feelings. Then you will think about who on the list you feel you can trust the most to help you with your SI. Finally, you will find a form that can help you communicate to any of these people what they can do or say to help you.

activity 21 ✳ talking with people about who you really are

with whom can you talk?

Think about people who care about you and with whom you can talk, and list them here:

1. _____

2. _____

3. _____

4. _____

5. _____

6. _____

7. _____

8. _____

9. _____

10. _____

All of the people on your list form your support system, the people who support your feelings and are committed to helping you be happier. Being supportive doesn't always mean that people will agree with you, but it does mean that they care deeply about you and respect you.

Now choose three people from your list that you feel most comfortable talking with about your thoughts and feelings. These people form your primary support system. Think about how you can contact each of these people and how they can best help give you the support you need.

Contact 1

Name _____

Phone number(s)_____

Best time to call_____

Can I call this person in an emergency?   Yes   No

Can I call late at night?   Yes   No

Can I call just to talk?   Yes   No

I can expect this person to always_____.

Other comments about this person: _____

_____

_____

_____

_____

Contact 2

Name _____

Phone number(s)_____

Best time to call_____

Can I call this person in an emergency?   Yes   No

Can I call late at night?   Yes   No

Can I call just to talk?   Yes   No

I can expect this person to always_____.

Other comments about this person: _____

_____

_____

_____

_____

_____

Contact 3

Name _____

Phone number(s)_____

Best time to call_____

Can I call this person in an emergency?   Yes   No

Can I call late at night?   Yes   No

Can I call just to talk?   Yes   No

I can expect this person to always_____.

Other comments about this person: _____

_____

_____

_____

_____

_____

You can use the form below to help people give you the kind of support you want. After you fill it in, you can talk to the people in your support system about it or you can give it to them to use as a guide. Remember that everyone can't treat you exactly as you like. Some people are better at giving support than others, but this exercise can help you think about the kinds of things that you need for support and hopefully get them.

how you can help me

The most important thing I need from you is _____

_____.

The one thing I don't want you to do is _____

_____.

I would like to talk with you at least _____ times a week.

The best place to talk is _____.

I would like to hear what you think, but I don't want you to _____

_____.

When I tell you things that are difficult for me to say, I would you like you to _____

_____.

Other things you can do to help me are _____

_____

_____

_____

_____.

thinking about yourself

Name one person you know who really understands how you feel when you are upset.

_____

What is it about this person that makes you feel this way? _____

_____

Is there someone you think might be more of a support for you in the future, if you were to ask for help?

_____

What prevents you from asking for help? _____

_____

_____

_____

22 your parents need to know how you are feeling

you need to know

Most teens who self-harm (and many who don't) say that they feel alone and that no one really understands their feelings. Many teens think their parents are not really interested in them and don't care about who they really are. Most parents do care a lot about their teens, but they often don't know how to say or do the things that would be really helpful.

While it is common for parents and teens to have a difficult time seeing each others' points of view, it is important to at least try to keep communication going. There may be many areas where parents and teens don't agree, but with effort, they can usually find compromises even if they just agree to disagree.

Teens who self-injure need the support of their parents. It is important that your parents hear about your feelings. This exercise gives you the chance to tell your parents about your feelings by simply filling in the blanks. You don't have to fill in all the sentences, just the ones you want to.

It is up to you whether you show this letter to your parents. There might be better ways to talk to your parents, such as in family counseling. Even if you choose not to talk to your parents at all about your feelings, you should still keep in mind this general principle: when you talk to people about how you feel, you are much more likely to get the support you need.

a letter to your parents

Dear _____ ,

I'm writing this letter to let you know more about me.

One thing that makes me really happy is _____.

One thing that makes me really sad is _____.

One thing that has troubled me for a long time is _____

_____.

It would help me if _____

_____.

One thing I wish I could change in my life is _____.

You can help me with this wish by _____

_____.

The person I feel I can trust most is _____.

One thing I wish you would never say to me is _____

_____.

One thing I wish you would always say to me is _____

_____.

Also, I want you to know _____

_____

_____

_____

_____

_____

_____

_____.

It helps me when you know how I feel. It helps me to know that you can accept my feelings, even though they may be hard for you to understand.

Love,

_____

thinking about yourself

Describe a time when you felt that your parents were very supportive of your feelings.

_____

_____

_____

What is the best time to talk with your father? How can you tell when it is a good time to talk with him?

_____

_____

_____

What is the best time to talk with your mother? How can you tell when it is a good time to talk with her?

_____

_____

_____

Is there another adult family member whom you can confide in and get support from?

_____

_____

23 telling your parents what they should or shouldn't say

you need to know

All teenagers complain that their parents do and say things that drive them crazy. Your parents may do things that make you feel bad about yourself, even when this is not their intention. There is no such thing as a perfect parent, but when you communicate more with your parents, it will be more likely that they can say and do things that are more supportive.

Everyone has certain hot buttons that really set them off. Many teens complain that their parents say exactly the wrong thing at the wrong time. Many parents complain that their teens are hard to talk with and often storm out of the room when they are trying to start a conversation. It is not easy to have an open and honest conversation with your parents, particularly if you have a history of misunderstanding each other, but it is worth the effort. If you feel that your parents are not really looking out for your best interests, you can find another family member, or even a friend of the family, who might act in place of your parents.

Many teens benefit from family therapy or from having their parents come to several sessions with their counselor. Having your therapist as an advocate will help you feel that you can say things to your parents that would otherwise be very difficult. Your counselor can also act as a mediator, helping you and your parents work out compromises and find better ways to communicate with each other.

On the next page, you will find statements about how you want your parents to react regarding your SI. Complete them as honestly as you can. You may want to talk to your therapist about whether you want to show the list to your parents. Your parents may need some support and counseling to help them react to you in the best way possible. Parents have their own problems, and not every parent can say or do exactly what their teens need. But if your parents will try to understand you and you will try to understand them, you will have made an important beginning.

how do you want your parents to react to your si?

Complete the statements below. Then add five things you would like your parents to know about how you want them to react.

If you see fresh scars or signs of self-injury, I want you to _____

_____

_____

_____.

If my teachers ask about my SI, I would like you to _____

_____

_____

_____.

If other family members ask about my SI, I would like you to _____

_____

_____

_____.

If I look sad or upset, I would like you to _____

_____

_____

_____.

activity 23 ✳ telling your parents what they should or shouldn't say

If I seem angry, I would like you to _____
_____
_____
_____.

These are some other things you can to do help me:

_____

_____

_____

_____

_____

_____

_____

_____

_____

thinking about yourself

Describe a time you had a great conversation with a parent or another adult.

_____

_____

Do you feel that you take your parents' views into consideration?

_____

_____

What is one thing that really sets your mother off?

_____

What is one thing that really sets your father off?

_____

When is the best time in the week to have a good conversation with one or both of your parents?

_____

_____

What is the best place (e.g., a room in your home, a restaurant, a park) to have a good conversation with one or both of your parents?

_____

_____

section 4

✳

conquering your si

In this section you will learn the skills you need to stop, or at least lessen, the emotional pain that is making you self-injure.

Everyone has emotional pain throughout life. It is something people simply have to accept. But as you progress toward recovery, you should feel more in control of the way you deal with your problems and you should find better ways to cope with difficult feelings. Certainly you should stop doing things that make your problems worse.

Recovering from any addictive behavior can take a long time. It may be several years before you feel that self-injury is no longer a problem in your life. But every step that you take should make your journey easier and lighten your emotional burden.

Most important, as you learn to conquer your SI, you should begin to feel happier about yourself and your life. No one can be happy all the time, but as you learn to deal with the problems that have led you to self-injure, you should find more and more moments when you feel safe, calm, and confident.

finding a safe place where you can stop hurting yourself 24

you need to know

Most teens who self-injure find that specific situations or events trigger the feelings that make them want to hurt themselves. These situations or events make them feel out of control and overwhelmed, and hurting themselves is the only way they know to calm themselves and feel back in control. Going to a safe place where you can feel calm and in control and have positive feelings about yourself will help you control your SI habit.

A safe place can be an actual place, or it can be a place in your mind. In this activity, you will think about creating a physical place where you can feel safe. In Activity 25: *Creating a Safe Place in Your Mind*, you will try to create a safe place in your mind to help you when you feel upset or out of control.

creating a safe place

Imagine you are creating a perfect space for yourself, where you could go to feel peaceful, calm, and positive. In the box below, draw the things that you would find there, such as a comfortable chair, a CD player, pictures or photographs, books, stuffed animals, and so on. On the right, make a list of all the things in your safe place.

Is it possible for you to actually create a place like this? Is there a place where you can have at least some of the things on your list?

_____

_____

Describe a place you can create today that makes you feel even a little safer.

_____

_____

_____

_____

_____

_____

_____

_____

creating a safe place in your mind 25

you need to know

When you are upset, it may impossible to go to an actual safe place, but you can create a place in your mind that will help you feel safer, calmer, and more in control.

Most teens who self-injure say that the urge to hurt themselves lasts for a relatively short time. People usually hurt themselves when they are overwhelmed by upsetting feelings, like guilt, shame, or anger. Using imagery to create a calm picture in your mind can help you control these difficult feelings and then do something that will make you feel better. Imagery is a powerful psychological tool. It is the basis for hypnosis, which many people have used to eliminate emotional, and even physical, pain.

Can you create an image of a safe place in your mind? It might be the beach at sunset, with waves splashing on the shore. Or it could be an image of you being hugged and cared for by a person important to you. Most people can easily create visual images, and many people can create sound images as well. It is harder to create images of smell, taste, or touch, but you might be able to do it. Your brain can store your sensory impressions as memories, although some people are better at recreating memories than others. The more senses you can use to create a safe place in your mind, the better you will feel.

In the space below, draw a safe place that you can carry around with you in your mind. If you prefer, you can use photographs and pictures from magazines.

When you are done, stare at this picture for one minute. Then close your eyes, trying to keep the picture in your mind, and add memories from your other senses.

thinking about yourself

How did you feel after you did the previous exercise? Write down all your feelings.

_____

_____

_____

How easy was it for you to concentrate on this image? Did you find that other thoughts or images started to intrude? What were they? _____

_____

_____

_____

Can you think of other images that might make you feel calmer and more in control? Write them here. _____

_____

_____

_____

Will you try using imagery when you feel like hurting yourself? If not, why not?

_____

_____

_____

26 setting goals for yourself will help you stop your si

you need to know

When people want to change a habit, they often set goals for themselves and decide on a period of time for meeting those goals. Setting goals and a time frame to reach your goals will make it easier to change your behavior.

When you decide to stop hurting yourself, you may find it helpful to set specific goals that can lead you to a healthier and happier life. In this activity, you will find a chart with some goals that you might want to work toward and a place to note the time when you hope to achieve these goals. There is also room for you to list obstacles that might come up while you are working toward your goals.

goals for people who self-injure

Some goals set by people with SI include the following:

- I will reduce my SI to _____ times per month.

- I will contact my counselor or another adult every time I feel like hurting myself.

- I will find a replacement activity for my SI and use it consistently.

- I will practice calming myself to deal with my emotions.

- I will avoid objects that I use to hurt myself.

- I will find a safe place to go when I feel like I need to hurt myself.

Here are some other goals that might help you:

- I will start an exercise program.

- I will reconnect with former friends.

- I will work harder in school.

- I will get involved in community service programs.

Write other goals that relate to your SI: _____

_____

_____

_____

_____

Write other goals that you want to set for yourself: _____

_____

_____

_____

Some obstacles that teens with SI encounter include the following:

- School stress

- Being hassled by parents or teachers

- Peer pressure

- Setbacks with a diet

- Physical illness

- Family changes

You may have encountered other obstacles as well. Write them below:

_____

_____

_____

_____

your recovery goal chart

It is important to write down your goals and keep track of your progress. Look at the goals and obstacles from the previous pages. Write your five most important goals in the chart below. Then fill in the date you started working toward the goal, the date you think it can be met, and any obstacles that might occur. Once the goal is achieved, use a scale from 1 to 5 to rate how successful you were, with 1 = "somewhat successful" and 5 = "very successful." For example, say that your goal is to exercise every day, and now you don't exercise at all. You hope to meet that goal in one month. But in a month, you are only exercising three times a week. You have worked toward your goal and changed your habits, and your success rating would be a 3.

Goal	Date Started	Date Goal Will Be Met	Obstacles That Might Occur	Date Goal is Achieved	Success Rating

thinking about yourself

Have you ever set goals for yourself before? Have you achieved them?

_____

_____

_____

Do you think you tend to set your goals too high, too low, or just right? Explain your thinking.

_____

_____

_____

When you made a list of the obstacles that might keep you from achieving your goals, did anything stand out? If so, what?

_____

_____

_____

What were the top three obstacles you listed? Is there anything that these obstacles have in common? Can you find a healthy way to overcome these obstacles?

_____

_____

_____

creating an si emergency kit 27

> ## you need to know
>
> Many people who self-injure find it useful to create an emergency kit, which is an actual box with contents that will help them when they feel they must self-injure.

These are some things you can put in your emergency kit:

- A list of people you can call

- A list of things you can do when you feel like hurting yourself (as in Activity 20)

- A journal to write your thoughts and feelings in

- A ball, such as a tennis ball, you can squeeze to let out your tensions

- A CD or tape of soothing music

- A photograph of someone you care about

List some other things you can put in your emergency kit.

_____

_____

_____

_____

_____

thinking about yourself

What do you think would be the most useful items in your emergency kit?

_____

_____

_____

What might prevent you from using your emergency kit?

_____

_____

_____

Can you carry your emergency kit with you? If your answer is yes, how can you make certain to do it? If your answer is no, explain your answer.

_____

_____

Feeling that you are going to self-injure would be one reason to have an emergency kit. Can you think of other emotional emergencies that this kit might be used for? Write them below.

_____

_____

_____

coping with stress 28

you need to know

Everyone experiences some stress every day. The more ways you can find to cope with stress, the happier and healthier you will be.

Stress can come from something little, like having a "bad hair day" or a hangnail that bothers you. When you have a test or have to go to a big family event, you may experience more stress. Even good things can cause stress. Going to a party can be stressful for some teens, even when they expect to have fun. Then there are big things that cause stress: a divorce, a serious illness, being teased or bullied, arguing with a friend, a relationship breaking up, or moving to another town. You have probably had many things happen to you that have been very stressful.

Stress causes your brain to produce a chemical called cortisol. Cortisol is one of the many brain chemicals that controls the way we feel and act. When your brain produces a little cortisol, like just before a test, you feel alert and in control. But when you have a lot of stress, your brain produces too much cortisol, and this can make you physically ill, depressed, or anxious.

Some teens hurt themselves when they feel stressed. They say that they actually feel they can control their stress more when they self-injure. But then their feelings of embarrassment or shame about hurting themselves cause stress, too, so that they end up feeling even worse and more out of control.

When you find better ways to deal with stress, you can learn to control the feelings that make you want to self-injure, and you can break this addictive habit.

There are many healthy ways to cope with stress, including the following:

- Talking to friends and family

- Exercise, particularly sports that involve other people

- Creative activities like music, dance, or art

- Relaxation activities

Relaxation activities are one of the best ways to cope with stress. These can include yoga, deep breathing, or just listening to restful music. Watching television or even reading a book have not been suggested as ways to cope with stress, because these activities distract you but don't really lower your stress level. Things that reduce your stress actually change the way your body works by lowering your heart rate and blood pressure and reducing the levels of cortisol in your brain while producing the chemicals that will make you feel better, such as endorphins and serotonin.

In this activity, you will think about different ways to cope with stress by relaxing. Learning to relax when you are stressed isn't that easy. Like most things you learn, it takes practice. For one week, choose a time during the day when you can take ten or fifteen minutes to relax. Then use the chart on the next page to rate how successful you were at relaxing for the entire week.

Remember that the more you practice stress-reduction techniques, the easier it will be to cope with stress.

relaxation log

Week of _____

Day and Time	What You Did to Relax	Minutes of Relaxation	How You Felt After Relaxing (Rate on a 1-10 scale with 1 = "very stressed" and 10 = "peaceful and calm")

List all of the different activities that help you relax: _____

_____

_____

_____

Which of these is most helpful in coping with stress? _____

_____

Which of these is most fun? _____

_____

Looking back at your log, what did you learn about your relaxation habits?

_____

_____

_____

What can you do to make relaxation a part of your daily life?

_____

_____

_____

you need to know

Many people find that mindfulness, a type of meditation, helps them feel more in control of their lives. Mindfulness means being aware of yourself and your surroundings. When you are mindful, you clear your head of distracting thoughts and you tune in to what you are experiencing at the moment. Practicing mindfulness can help you deal with difficult times in your life and resist the urge to self-injure.

Many counselors believe that mindfulness is an important tool in learning to overcome SI. Self-injury is a way of deadening your feelings and removing yourself from problems. Mindfulness tries to do the opposite. It is intended to make you aware of your feelings and your surroundings and to awaken your senses. When you are more aware of your feelings and your sensations, you will be able to find ways to feel good more of the time and to confront your problems directly. This is an important part of breaking the cycle of negative feelings that come before and after the times you self-injure.

The basic steps of learning to be mindful are simple:

1. Sit or lie quietly and notice your breath moving in and out.

2. Notice anything else you feel in your body.

3. As other thoughts intrude, let them go.

4. Remain aware of being in the present moment.

Practice being mindful several times a day, even for just a few minutes at a time. As the "chatter" in your mind settles, you should feel calm and discover a peaceful state.

Mindfulness takes practice, but when you learn it, you can apply it to many activities throughout your day. On the next page are some suggestions for times you can practice being mindful.

getting in the habit of being mindful

Practicing mindfulness for just few minutes a day can be a useful way to develop a sense of calm and confidence. Look at the list below and check two or three ways of being mindful that appeal to you. On the blank lines, you can write your own ideas for times and places where you can be mindful.

_____ Pay attention to your breathing or your environment when you are riding in a car.

_____ Before you go to sleep and when you wake up, take some "mindful" breaths. Instead of allowing your mind to wander over the day's concerns, direct your attention to your breathing.

_____ Find a task that you normally rush through, like brushing your teeth, and concentrate on the experience.

_____ Use something that occurs several times during a day, such as answering the phone or taking your seat in a classroom, as a reminder to think about what you're doing. Observe yourself doing it.

_____ Focus on your food, rather than watching TV or talking to someone while you eat.

_____ Stop to notice your breath at various times throughout the day.

_____

_____

_____

_____

_____

_____

thinking about yourself

How hard did you find it to be mindful? Do you think that this is a technique you can learn? If not, why not? _____

_____

_____

Multitasking, or doing several things at the same time, is the opposite of being mindful. What are some ways that you typically multitask during the day (for example, listening to music and doing your homework at the same time, talking on the phone while you are eating a meal)? _____

_____

_____

When you are able to be mindful, do you notice a difference in your feelings? How would you describe your feelings? _____

_____

_____

Do you find that it is hard to keep unwanted thoughts or feelings out of your head when you are trying to be mindful? What are some of the thoughts or feelings that intrude?_____

_____

_____

30 dealing with upsetting thoughts and feelings

you need to know

Many people who self-injure say that they hurt themselves to deaden difficult, upsetting feelings and memories. You may feel ashamed or guilty about something even if you really haven't done anything wrong. Feelings are not logical, and many people say that they often have upsetting feelings they can't explain.

Hopefully your therapist will help you learn to better understand your upsetting feelings and memories. But even before you understand them, you can learn to tolerate them. Many of the activities in this workbook can help you tolerate your upsetting feelings, using the following techniques:

	Activity Number
Changing the automatic thoughts associated with a disturbing thought or memory	17
Increasing your positive and pleasant experiences	18
Finding replacement activities	20
Talking to others	21
Relaxing	28
Being mindful	29
Having a healthy lifestyle	34
Praying	36

In this activity, you will learn more about how your upsetting thoughts, feelings, and memories affect you and what you can do that will be effective in coping with them.

rating your upsetting thoughts and feelings

Not all the things that upset you are equal. In this exercise, you should write down five thoughts or memories that upset you and the feelings they trigger. In the third column, rate them from 1 to 5, with 1 = "least upsetting" and 5 = "most upsetting." In the fourth column, rate how often you have these feelings, with 1 = "seldom" and 5 = "almost every day."

Thoughts That Upset You	Feelings They Trigger	How Much They Upset You	How Often You Have These Feelings

thinking about yourself

Are there specific situations that cause you to have upsetting feelings?

_____

_____

_____

Most teens say that they self-injure as a way to deal with upsetting feelings. Are there other ways that you try to numb yourself from upsetting thoughts and feelings, like using drugs or alcohol?

_____

_____

_____

Have you developed any healthy ways to deal with upsetting thoughts or memories?

_____

_____

_____

Are there thoughts and memories which used to bother you that you have learned to cope with? Write them here.

_____

_____

_____

what triggers your upsetting thoughts and behaviors? 31

you need to know

Many people don't really know what makes them suddenly feel upset. All of a sudden, they are simply overwhelmed by feelings like helplessness, anxiety, guilt, shame, sadness, or even despair. Learning to understand the things that trigger your thoughts, feelings, and self-destructive behaviors will be an important step on your road to recovery.

The emotional part of our brains (the limbic system) does not work in logical fashion. We often don't know why we have disturbing thoughts that trigger feelings that cause discomfort and then cause us to behave in self-destructive ways. There are times when thoughts and feelings do not follow any observable logical pattern. This can be due to a chemical imbalance in the brain caused by drugs, inherited genetic factors, or even environmental pollutants. Trauma, including physical or sexual abuse, can cause people to think upsetting thoughts or have vague, upsetting feelings without being aware of where they come from. But even when our thoughts are not logical, they do follow a pattern. Most of the time there is some trigger, or cue, that precedes an upsetting thought.

identifying triggers for your upsetting thoughts

On this line, write the most upsetting thought you listed on page 115:

_____

Every time you have this thought, write down other things that are happening. After one week, review this chart and determine if there are recurring triggers (time, people, places, situations, or events) for your upsetting thought. You can repeat this activity for other thoughts that disturb you.

Time of Day	People Around You	Place	Situation or Event

thinking about yourself

What kinds of things most often trigger your upsetting thoughts? _____

_____

_____

Are there combinations of factors that trigger these thoughts? _____

_____

_____

What changes can you make in your life to change the things that trigger your upsetting thoughts or feelings? _____

_____

_____

32 desensitizing yourself to your upsetting thoughts and feelings

you need to know

Some thoughts and feelings are very powerful. Some people say that their fears, anxieties, and feelings of shame and guilt take over their whole lives. But it doesn't have to be this way. Psychologists have found a way to lessen even the most powerful feelings through a process called desensitization. If you practice desensitization techniques, you can more easily deal with the things that upset you.

Desensitization is a common psychological technique used to treat a variety of problems. The word means just what it sounds like—reducing your sensitivity or reactivity to thoughts, memories, or feelings.

There are three steps to desensitization:

1. Relaxation

2. Prioritizing your upsetting thoughts and feelings

3. Pairing relaxation with your upsetting thoughts and feelings

Desensitization is often used with people who have specific fears, like flying, being in closed-in places, or crossing bridges. Using this technique, people learn to approach their fears in small steps, calming their minds and bodies at each step. You can use this same method to diminish the upsetting feelings that precede your self-injury. When you learn that you can control these feelings, you will find it much easier to stop your SI.

On the following page, you will find the steps for desensitizing yourself to the upsetting thoughts and feelings connected to your SI.

desensitizing yourself to your upsetting thoughts and feelings

Before you begin, make at least five copies of the Desensitization Rating Log on the next page.

1. Write down five of the situations or events from the chart on page 115. Use a separate index card for each.

2. Find a comfortable place to sit and try to relax your mind and body as much as possible. Breathe deeply and relax all your muscles. You can also use the relaxation activities from page 109.

3. Pick up one card and read it to yourself. Think about the situation or event and imagine that you are there. Do this for just three minutes. If you have a timer, use it to keep track of the minutes.

4. Stop! On the chart that follows, rate how upset you were, with 1 = "not upset at all" and 10 = "my feelings were intolerable."

5. Reread the card and imagine the situation or event again for approximately four minutes.

6. Now rate your feelings again, using the rating scale in step 4.

7. Continue doing this two more times, increasing the time you think about the situation or event first to five minutes and then to seven minutes.

8. Now go back and look at your ratings. Were you able to keep your upsetting feelings below a 3? If not, keep practicing this desensitization exercise, using the same card.

9. If you were able to keep your upsetting feelings at 3 or below, go on to the next card, using a new copy of the Desensitization Rating Log.

10. Practice this exercise once a day until you find it easy to keep your upsetting feelings under control.

desensitization rating log

Situation _____

Time Interval	Rating	Comments
3 minutes		
4 minutes		
5 minutes		
7 minutes		

thinking about yourself

Do you feel that you have more control over your feelings after completing the desensitization activity? _____

_____

Do you find that calming your upsetting feelings gets easier with practice? If not, what do you think is preventing you from getting control of your feelings? _____

_____

_____

Do you think that you can use this desensitization technique with actual situations rather than ones you are thinking about? If not, why not? _____

_____

_____

List five situations where you could use relaxation techniques to slowly desensitize yourself, a few minutes at a time, to the upsetting feelings that the situation usually brings up.

1. _____

2. _____

3. _____

4. _____

5. _____

33 facing your problems around food

you need to know

Many teens who self-injure also have emotional problems with food. They may starve themselves by eating too little or they may binge-eat and then throw up or they may overeat when they are upset. If you have an eating disorder or a problem with food, then you should assume that it is related to the same emotional problems that have caused your SI. When you develop a healthier attitude toward food and toward your body image, you will be further along on your road to recovery.

Many people feel that eating disorders are simply another way that people hurt their bodies. In fact, people with severe eating disorders do cause physical pain to themselves. The activities in this workbook can help you better understand how you handle emotional problems, which can, in turn, help you develop a healthier lifestyle.

To begin, you should consider whether or not you have a problem with food. The questionnaire on page 125 will help you determine whether you need to change your attitude and behavior around food as part of your recovery plan.

food questionnaire

Do you feel pressure to be thin?	____ yes	____ no
Do you feel that you are not attractive if you are not thin ?	____ yes	____ no
Are you preoccupied with food?	____ yes	____ no
Do you feel guilty about eating?	____ yes	____ no
Do you feel that you are never satisfied with the way that you look?	____ yes	____ no
Do you constantly think about your weight and what you eat?	____ yes	____ no
Do you diet excessively?	____ yes	____ no
Do you abuse laxatives, diuretics, or diet pills?	____ yes	____ no
Do you prefer eating alone?	____ yes	____ no
Do you count the calories in every bite you eat?	____ yes	____ no
Do you turn to food when you are feeling low?	____ yes	____ no
Do you ever feel that you are out of control when you eat?	____ yes	____ no
Do you try to vomit after you think you have eaten too much?	____ yes	____ no
Do you feel that you would be happier if you were thinner?	____ yes	____ no
Do you constantly compare your body and appearance to others?	____ yes	____ no
Do family members or friends seem concerned about your weight?	____ yes	____ no
Do you keep your concerns about food a secret?	____ yes	____ no
Do you lie about what you have eaten?	____ yes	____ no

If you have answered yes to two or more of these questions, you may have a problem with food. If you have answered yes to more than five of these questions, you may have an eating disorder or be at risk for developing one. This is something that you need to talk about with your counselor, as part of your recovery plan.

thinking about yourself

Did any of your answers to the Food Questionnaire surprise you? _____

_____

_____

Have you ever thought of yourself as having an eating disorder before? If so, what have you done about it? _____

_____

_____

On a scale of 1 to 10, how would you rate your problems around food, with 1 = "not serious" and 10 = "life threatening?" _____

What steps are you going to take to deal with your problems around food? List them here.

_____

_____

_____

_____

_____

_____

do you have a healthy lifestyle?

you need to know

Many people don't think much about what they eat during the day. You may think that you don't have a problem with food, but the only way to really find out is to record what you eat for several days. You should also know that the food you eat has an important effect on the biochemicals in your brain that control your moods. When you eat a healthy diet, your brain will produce more of the biochemicals that help you feel calm and in control.

You probably know that a balanced diet includes protein, fruits, vegetables, and carbohydrates. Foods high in sugar and fats are not considered to be part of a healthy diet and may cause you to have energy high and lows throughout the day.

Getting a good night's sleep (at least eight hours) and exercising every day will also help your brain produce biochemicals that will improve your mood.

As part of your recovery plan, you should try to live a healthier life. The more you pay attention to having a healthier lifestyle, the less you will feel like hurting yourself.

food and behavior log

Make several copies of this log. At the end of the day, write down what you have eaten and how much you exercised. You should also indicate what your mood was throughout the day, noting whether it varied according to the time of day or the food you ate.

Day and Date _____   Hours of Sleep I Got Last Night _____

Time	What I Ate	Exercise (in minutes)	My Mood

Rate how healthy you think your lifestyle was on this day, using 1 = "poor" and 5 = "very healthy."

Your Rating _____

thinking about yourself

Who do you know that lives a healthy lifestyle? What motivates this person?

_____

_____

What are some things that keep you from eating a healthier diet? _____

_____

_____

What are some things that keep you from exercising more often? _____

_____

_____

Here are some ways that you can improve your eating and exercise habits. Put a check mark next to the ones that you think you may use to help you develop a healthier lifestyle.

_____ Join a gym.

_____ Join a sports team.

_____ Take up jogging.

_____ Keep a food log.

_____ Consult a nutritionist.

_____ Talk to a counselor about my problems around eating.

_____ Join Weight Watchers or another diet group.

_____ Cut significantly down on junk food.

_____ Talk to my parents about serving healthier food at home.

_____ Get help with any sleeping problems by talking to my counselor or physician.

35 facing problems with drugs and alcohol

you need to know

Many people who self-injure use drugs and alcohol to escape from their unhappiness and deaden their feelings. If you take drugs or drink alcohol and you want to stop, consider joining a 12-Step program.

As you know, many teens experiment with drugs and alcohol. You are undoubtedly aware of all the dangers associated with drugs and alcohol and don't need another lecture on this subject. But if you take drugs or drink alcohol, it's important for you to think about how this behavior is related to your SI and to your overall emotional and physical health.

You may think that using drugs is a better way of dealing with problems than injuring yourself, but drugs and alcohol are just other ways to avoid dealing with problems. For many teens who self-injure, drugs and alcohol make SI an even more dangerous behavior.

On page 131, you'll find a list of drugs commonly used by teens and the health consequences of using these drugs, based on information from the National Institute on Drug Abuse. Take a few minutes to read through the list of drugs and their possible effects.

Drug	Possible Effects
Marijuana, hash	slowed thinking and reaction time; confusion; impaired balance and coordination; cough; frequent respiratory infections; impaired memory and learning; increased heart rate; anxiety; panic attacks; tolerance; addiction
Barbiturates	poor concentration; fatigue; confusion; impaired coordination, memory, and judgment; addiction; respiratory depression or arrest; sedation; drowsiness; depression; unusual excitement; fever; irritability; slurred speech; dizziness; life-threatening withdrawal; death
PCP	delirium; depression; respiratory depression or arrest; decrease in blood pressure and heart rate; panic; aggression; violence; loss of appetite
LSD (and hallucinogenics)	altered states of perception and feeling; nausea; flashbacks; increased body temperature, heart rate, or blood pressure; loss of appetite; sleeplessness; numbness; weakness; tremors
Opiates (heroin, codeine, Oxycontin, morphine)	nausea; constipation; confusion; sedation; respiratory depression or arrest; tolerance; addiction; unconsciousness; coma; death
Amphetamines	rapid or irregular heart beat; reduced appetite; weight loss; heart failure; nervousness; insomnia
Cocaine	rapid breathing; tremor; loss of coordination; irritability; anxiousness; restlessness; delirium; panic; paranoia; impulsive behavior; aggressiveness; tolerance; addiction; psychosis
Ecstasy	impaired memory and learning; hyperthermia; cardiac toxicity; renal failure; liver toxicity
Ritalin (methylphenidate)	aggression; violence; psychotic behavior; memory loss; cardiac and neurological damage; impaired memory and learning; tolerance; addiction
Nicotine	chronic lung disease; cardiovascular disease; stroke; cancer; addiction
Inhalants	unconsciousness; cramps; weight loss; muscle weakness; depression; memory impairment; damage to cardiovascular and nervous systems; sudden death

thinking about yourself

How often have you been under the influence of drugs when you self-injured?

_____

_____

How many of your friend abuse drugs and alcohol? _____

_____

Have you ever tried to quit taking drugs or drinking alcohol? What happened?

_____

_____

Are you ready to make a commitment to deal with a drug or alcohol habit? If not, why not?

_____

_____

_____

spiritual faith may help you 36
stop self-injury

you need to know

Many people find that a belief in a higher power can help them stop hurting themselves and give them a positive direction in their lives. This is particularly true of people who feel that their self-destructive behaviors are beyond their control.

Churches, synagogues, or other places of worship often have have special programs for teens. These programs can give you a new way to look at yourself and new, positive emotions, including faith, hope, and trust. But even if you don't practice a formal religion or attend religious services, you can still have a belief in a higher power.

Many people find inspiration and renewal in believing that God or some higher power will listen to their prayers and guide them to seek a life full of meaning. Others feel that prayer is more like meditation; its value is in helping them clarify their thoughts and focus their feelings in a positive way. Whatever your faith and whatever your beliefs, you may find that prayer and meditation can be an important part of your road away from self-injury, depression, and pain.

On the next page is an activity that asks you to write your personal prayer. Try this activity, even if you don't believe in God or a higher power. Say your personal prayer every day for two weeks and notice whether it makes a difference in your thoughts and feelings about your life.

your personal prayer

Dear God,

What I really need in my life is _____.

Please give me the wisdom to _____.

The most important thing I need to do is _____.

Please give me the strength to _____.

I promise _____.

I am so grateful that _____.

And I hope and pray that _____.

Thank you for your blessings.

Amen

are you prepared to stop 37
self-injury?

you need to know

This workbook was designed to help you think about the reasons that you hurt yourself and to develop new behaviors that will help you find better ways to cope with your emotional problems. If you are ready to completely stop your SI, you need to be prepared.

Hopefully, the activities in this workbook, along with the work you are doing with your counselor, have helped you significantly reduce the number of times you self-injure. Are you now ready to stop hurting yourself completely?

On the next page is a form to help you be prepared to stop hurting yourself for the rest of your life. The more statements that are true of you, the more you will be prepared to stop your SI.

preparing to stop your si

Check off the statements that are true:

_____ It is very important to me to stop hurting myself.

_____ I have told the important people in my life about my SI.

_____ I have at least two people I can call when I want to hurt myself.

_____ I know the feelings that I get before I hurt myself.

_____ I know the situations that trigger my self-injury.

_____ I know the thoughts that trigger my self-injury.

_____ I have gotten rid of the things that I use to hurt myself.

_____ I have a list of things I can to do instead of hurting myself.

_____ I have a place where I can go to feel safe when I feel like hurting myself.

_____ I am in therapy with a counselor who I trust to help me stop my SI for good.

thinking about yourself

Making a commitment to stop hurting yourself is a big step. Do you feel proud of yourself for doing this? _____

_____

Changing any habit is difficult. What is one thing that you think will get in the way of your recovering from self-injury? _____

_____

Were there any statements that you were not able to check off on page 136? In the space below, write about what you can do to further prepare yourself to stop your SI for good.

_____

_____

_____

_____

_____

38 reviewing what you have learned about your si

you need to know

Now that you are almost done with this workbook, it is time to reflect on what you have learned. Reviewing what you have learned on a regular basis will help reinforce your healthy thoughts and behaviors.

These are the top ten things you can learn from this workbook:

1. You can control the upsetting emotions that lead to your SI.

2. You can find replacement activities when you feel like hurting yourself.

3. You can change the thoughts that trigger your depression and your SI.

4. You can develop a better body image.

5. You can develop a healthier lifestyle.

6. You can form a network of friends, including adults, that you can turn to when you are upset.

7. You can develop an emergency plan to use when you are in a crisis.

8. You can overcome other problems related to your SI, like eating disorders and drug and alcohol abuse.

9. You can develop a better relationship with your parents, based on open communication.

10. You can be happier and find more pleasure in your life every day.

In doing these activities, you may also have learned other things about yourself and your SI. On the next page, make a list of the most important things you have learned. Just put down the ones that come to your mind as you are writing; you can always add to this list at a later time.

activity 38 ✳ reviewing what you have learned about your si

the things I have learned about my si

_____

_____

_____

_____

_____

_____

_____

_____

_____

_____

_____

_____

_____

_____

_____

thinking about yourself

What is the most helpful thing you have learned about your SI? _____

_____

_____

What is the most important thing you have learned about yourself, not related to your SI? _____

_____

Setbacks are common when you are trying to change something important about yourself. What is the most important thing you can do if you have a setback?

_____

_____

Ask someone who knows you well to tell you two things about you that have changed for the better in the last few months. Before you ask, write what you think they will say.

_____

_____

you can help yourself by 39
helping others

you need to know

Many people with problems find that, as they get better, they are ready to help others with the same problem. Helping others is an important way to reinforce your personal growth and your sense of purpose.

There are many ways that you can help other teens deal with problems similar to yours, or perhaps you would prefer to find ways to help people with other kinds or problems through community service. Here are some ways that you can help others:

- Enrolling in a peer counseling program where you will be trained to help other teens

- Tutoring younger children in academic subjects

- Being a Big Sister or Big Brother to a younger child

- Joining a support group for people with similar problems

- Community service activities (such as websites like www.pointsoflight.org that can help you find ways to volunteer in your area)

When you make helping others a part of your life, you will find that you add immeasurably to your sense of self-worth.

what can you teach others about dealing
with their emotional problems?

In the space below, write five things you have learned that you think would be beneficial to other teens.

1. _____

2. _____

3. _____

4. _____

5. _____

Write five ways that you can help other people in your community.

1. _____

_____

2. _____

_____

3 _____

_____

4. _____

_____

5. _____

_____

thinking about yourself

Have you ever done any kind of community service in the past? Why did you stop?

_____

_____

Do you know any groups that do community service, like church groups or school service clubs? Make a list of the ones you know about. _____

_____

_____

_____

Is there anything that might prevent you from taking time each week to reach out to others? _____

_____

Who do you know that is very involved community service? What motivates this person?_____

_____

_____

Lawrence E. Shapiro, Ph.D., is a nationally recognized child psychologist. His practical approach to helping kids and teens has been featured on radio, TV, and in national magazines.